ENCOUNTERING THE GLORY *of* GOD

DIANE NUTT

The *Joys* of Freedom Ministries
Publishing Division

Encountering The Glory of God
Copyright © 2018 by Diane Nutt
Edited by: Diane Nutt and Grayce Joy
Book Cover by: Yvette Ingram
Published by: The Joys of Freedom Ministries, Publishing Division, Hayden, Idaho 83835

All Rights Reserved. No part of this book may be reproduced, stored in a retrieval system, or transmitted in any form or by any means—electronic, mechanical, digital, photocopy, recording or any other—except the brief quotations in printed review, without the prior written permission from Diane Nutt.

ISBN-13: 978-153237025-0
ISBN-10: 153237025

All scripture quotations, unless otherwise indicated, are from the Authorized King James Version. All Rights Reserved. Words of Jesus in **bold**.

Printed in the United States of America

DEDICATION

This book is affectionately dedicated to my deceased mother, Nola Jean Brumbaugh, who shaped my life through her prayers and how she lived her life. She truly was a saint, one who never complained about anything and was always helping and doing for others. She always told me that she loved me, that she loved my husband, my children and was always praying for us.

Thank you, Mother, for always being there for me and for always praying for me. I love you more than I could ever put into words. Your last words to me on this earth was, "I love you!" They greatly impacted my heart. You revealed

God's Glory to me! I so look forward to Heaven, where I will see you again and we will never be separated.

This book is also dedicated to my best friend, my husband, Kenneth Nutt, who has always encouraged me that I can do whatever God calls me to do. You have always believed in me and at times, more than I have believed in my own self! I am so very grateful for you! As I said in my first book, This Nutt's Path To Freedom, I will always love you forever! You are solid and established in all you do! Thank you for being my friend, also, for being like a cheerleader in my corner. Encouraging me to keep moving forward! I love you dearly!

Last, but certainly not the least by any means, I dedicate this book and everything thing I do in my life to my Lord and Savior, Jesus Christ! Without You, I can do nothing. Without

You, life would not be worth living. You have given me Abundant Life so that I can live an Abundant life, forever giving You the Honor and Glory! You are my everything, my life and the very air that I breathe! My words cannot articulate my love for You and my heart is inadequate in conveying to You, my love for You! I love you for all eternity! I am forever Yours, as You are forever mine!

ENDORSEMENTS

When Diane Nutt speaks, the tangible Glory of God comes on the scene. I feel that same presence even on her text messages. Because of the brokenness and hunger for God, she has become a pioneer in the last and biggest display of God's Glory in history. As you read this book, you too, will experience the greater Glory.

—Sid Roth
Host, *It's Supernatural!*

Have you ever read a book that excites and invites you for a deeper commitment to the

Lord? This new book from Apostle Diane Nutt is that book! It is a clear, sound and powerful word filled with revelation that will ignite your hunger for God.

The heart's desire of the Father is to fellowship with us in a real way, manifesting Himself to His people. This timely book gives wonderful spiritual foundation for the encounters God wants you to have. Empowering your faith to draw near and to experience the manifest Glory of God. It is time for the body of Christ to experience new realms of God's Glory.

The life and ministry of Apostle Diane Nutt can be summed up in what the Apostle Paul said, "I come not with enticing words of man's wisdom and knowledge, but in demonstration of the power, gifting's of the Holy Spirit."

In conclusion, you will love this book and will want to personally experience the things of God.

—V.O. Stuart
Minister of the gospel of Christ

I've been around Apostle Diane Nutt about twenty-two years. She is a mighty woman of God. A woman after God's own heart. A true and real Apostle of God living and breathing the presence of the Glory of God. She always honors God and give Him the Glory. She never takes any Glory for herself.

Every time she worships and ministers, the Presence and Glory of God shows up. There's either a white cloud or a gold cloud over the top part of her body. Sometimes, she disappears in the cloud. As the Cloud of God's Glory appears; signs, wonders and miracles start happening. People start to see the Glory of God. They get saved, healed, delivered and set free. I'm one of those people that has seen the Glory of God manifested in her services. Time and time again I've seen it and my life has been changed and healed from being in the Glory of God manifested through Apostle Nutt's life.

I believe as you read this book, you will see the Glory of God. Your life will never be the same too!

"Thank you, Apostle Diane Nutt, for being faithful and obedient to the call of God on your life!"

—Gena Evans
Administrator
Church of His Glory

CONTENTS

Foreword 17
Acknowledgments 25
Introduction 29

CHAPTER ONE
Rejected and Abandoned 35

CHAPTER TWO
New Creatures in Christ 55

CHAPTER THREE
Sold Out to God 63

CHAPTER FOUR
God's Glory Manifested in Darkness 75

CHAPTER FIVE
God's Glory Lingers 83

CHAPTER SIX
A Changed Heart for Souls 93

CHAPTER SEVEN
Manifesting God's Glory 109

CHAPTER EIGHT
To Walk in Truth or Not 123

CHAPTER NINE
The Finger of God 135

CHAPTER TEN
The Secret Place 141

CHAPTER ELEVEN
Scriptures 153

About the Author 159

Another Book by Diane Nutt. 163

Soon to be Released Books 165

Contact Information. 168

FOREWORD

I saw and met Apostle Diane Nutt in 1994 at a church I attended in the state of Illinois. Little did I know what would transpire after that encounter with the Glory of God in her life. One point during the service, Apostle Nutt began to manifest the Joy of the Lord in laughing. The joy began to roll through the congregation in waves. People were laughing so hard they fell to the floor. The Joy of the Lord was evident, and this was a manifestation of the Glory of God I had never seen before or knew existed. I remember saying to the Lord within my spirit, "Lord, I want what she has, I want to know you like she does." Since that time, I've been blessed, honored and humbled by God to encounter and receive impartations of the Glory of God through Apostle Diane Nutt's life.

I've seen the Glory of God draw cattle to a fence when Apostle Diane only spoke the words "Hello" in a soft voice through the window on the passenger side as she was the driver and I was the passenger. All the cattle stopped eating and began walking towards the vehicle and we were on the road away from the cattle.

I watched as a dying butterfly, on the porch of our church was gently encouraged through Apostle Nutt talking to it, to walk over to her to gain rest. The butterfly made it over to her and got up under the insole of her shoe and rested there for a moment. The butterfly's wings started going up and down slowly. After going up and down slowly several times, it began to move its wings at a faster pace. And then the butterfly moved them more and more, faster and faster! Then it flew straight up past us into a strong headwind and was gone! The Glory of God that came through Apostle Nutt's voice healed that butterfly! I've seen people who have been driven back and pinned to a wall when they've tried to come near the Glory of God that protects Apostle Diane and they could not move until she left the area.

I've experienced the miraculous as it manifested in the Glory of God and saw people who could not walk without help from a walker and then saw them walk out without any assistance. Glory to God!! A woman came into the Glory of God with the diagnosis of cancer and her prognosis was not good. She was not given a long time to live. She left knowing that she had been healed from being in the Glory and came back the following month testifying that she was cancer free! Another woman came in deaf and after being in the Glory, when Apostle Diane prayed for her, she received her miracle, being able to hear. The Glory of God in Apostle Diane Nutt's life is very tangible in ways that only those hungry for God can fully experience. There have been many times when Apostle Diane did not pray for people and healings manifested. I have been one those people. I was in a service and the Glory of God was present, my head was hurting from being sick and without being prayed for, I left the service that morning with no more pain in my head.

When she walks in a room, the atmosphere immediately changes because of the Glory of God. Also, the fragrance of the Lord fills the atmosphere and the Life of Christ is released. I have encountered the Glory of God in Apostle Diane's life since 1994 and it has set me free from sexual perversion, many demonic oppressions, healed my ears, my stomach issues, depression; my sons have been transformed, my heart has been healed from emotional, physical, sexual, spiritual and financial abuse. Many of these deliverances came without Apostle Diane ever saying a word, just being in the presence of the Glory of God, I am changed forever. The Love of God that emanates from His glorious presence in Apostle Diane's life is truly life changing. I've never in my life experienced the depth of God's love being in His Glory anywhere else. There's billows of gentleness, peace, gratefulness, joy, hope, encouragement, strength, wholeness, whatever you need…it flows from the Glory of God in Apostle Diane's life and you are captivated in your heart and feel these things as you are encountering God's Glory. There's no place I'd rather be.

I've seen the Glory of God cover Apostle Diane to where I could not see her. I could only hear her voice and when these encounters have happened, God has always moved in my life to bring about revelation of a deliverance I was unaware I needed. There were many times where I would see a golden colored light surrounding her and it would intensify as she would be ministering the Word of God. Apostle Diane is the most loving, forgiving, humblest, honest, kindest, gentlest, caring, encouraging, longsuffering, patient, faith filled & faithful, peaceful, easy going, Holy Ghost fire filled, passionate worshiper, lover of Jesus, willing, obedient, repentant; glory living, walking and manifesting servants of God I know. She gives away whatever the Father pours into her life for people and she continually lays her life down for the Glory of God.

There's a fire that manifest from the Glory of God in Apostle Diane's life. It makes your flesh uncomfortable because it's so pure and holy.

FOREWORD

You know God is revealing something to you. In these moments, I know that God is searching my heart to let me know what I need to change. I am grateful for this pure, holy fire! The fire will burn up everything in my life that is not of God if I am willing and I am willing. It will do the same for you too! I'm hungry for God in my life and I am willing to do whatever it takes to know Him and see Him. The fire that manifests from the Glory of God in Apostle Diane's life is more of the Love of God being released through her life in the Glory. The Glory of God in her life is real, raw, powerful, holy, pure, tangible and life changing.

The Glory of God in her life has increased tremendously over the past twenty plus years that I have known her. So much to the point that whenever I speak with her, I feel God's Glory and His Holy Fire.

I truly believe that when you read about the encounters of God's Glory in Apostle Diane's life in this book, it will create a hunger in you for the Glory of God to manifest in and through you. I can tell you that is has for me. It has changed my life and it will change your life, too!

—Yvette Ingram
Teacher, Prophetic Intercessor, M.S., B.S., A.S.

ACKNOWLEDGMENTS

First and most importantly; I would like to give God all the Glory and Honor and Praise for anointing me to write this book. The words came so easy. I am so humbled for the life I have been given. I am so grateful for His mercy and goodness that follows me every day of my life. I feel so honored and privileged to be a Forerunner, a Pioneer that has made and is making the way for others. God does choose the foolish things to confound the wise. I would have never in my life imagined that God would give me the life that He has and then allow me to share it with others, like you, to help on this journey called life. As I said in my first book, **This Nutt's Path to Freedom**, that I wrote, *"If you can use anything Lord, use me!"*

I want to affectionately thank my husband, Kenneth, from the bottom of my heart. Thank you for your continual support of God's work and ministry in my life. You have encouraged me so many years in my life to write the books in my heart. You have never given up on me in aspiring me with my dreams. You have always been so confident in God in me to do whatever He has called me to do. It would be remiss for me to not say this again about you and me. You do you and I do me!! I love that about Us! Together, we are a force to be reckoned with! I'm so grateful that God allowed me to be your *"good thing"* that you found according to the Word of God! I love you! Always and Forever!

I'm so grateful that God will bless us with a true friend! I would rather have one, true friend than a whole room full of fake friends! Praise God for my dear friend, Yvette. She is a very gifted artist with other gifts and talents, but most of all, a

ACKNOWLEDGMENTS

heart of gold! Thank you for your willingness to yield yourself to the Master Artist to release through you the artistry to do the book cover for this book. I am forever grateful to God for you and your commitment. Thank you dearly!

Last, be not least, I would like to thank my Editor-In-Chief and Book Publisher who are the same, Grayce Linda Joy! It's been such a delight in knowing you and seeing the Fruit of our God-Ordained relationship since October of 2017. I love how Holy Spirit orchestrates our lives and brings all the notes together to make a beautiful song! Who would have ever thought or planned being a person in a meeting where someone was ministering; that over twenty plus years later, you would have a relationship with each other? Wow!! That's how God works, doing things that we wouldn't consider or come up with most of the time. I know I might sound redundant…I still want to thank you from the bottom of my heart for being a person that has such an incredible heart to help authors, like myself, to get our God given messages out! You are a jewel in the Kingdom of God, yet to be displayed as you will be in this Move of God that we have stepped into at this time! Thank you again so much!

INTRODUCTION

It is truly my honor and privilege to write this book and present it to you, the reader, for such a time as this. If you are reading this book, you are an answer to my prayer. As I have prayed for those of you who are hungry to know and encounter the Glory of God. Many have asked, "What is the Glory of God?" There have been many things that I have heard answered as to what the Glory of God is and most of what I have heard has not been what God has shown/taught me throughout the years. The Glory of God is not feathers, jewels, and gold dust! Although, God does not have a problem at all manifesting those things and delights in doing so for us, His children. They have never been a focus in my life, as I did not know about these manifestations until I was older. But these things did manifest in my life without me ever asking for them. I have been grateful every single time they have manifested in my life. I have always sought God and wanted more of Him in my life! Those other things just show up unannounced and I am so surprised when they do. If I'm around others, they always notice it before I do!

I don't claim to have a patent on the Glory of God, of course, but I do know a few things about the Glory of God that I have experienced for many years that others whom I know haven't. I want to take you on a journey of my life and share with you many things that I have encountered throughout the years concerning the Glory of God. But, I don't want to just share my stories with you. I want you, the reader, to know that there is another realm of Faith and another realm of Glory for you to step into as the Word of God says. My prayer is that you will be overtaken by the Presence of God as you read this book and the Glory of God will show up! Wherever you are and whatever you are doing, I believe that God will meet you at the place you are and reveal Himself to you, if you are hungry for Him! Just know that if you are pretending to be in a place with God that you are not, He cannot meet you there. It's totally okay to be you! Be real to yourself, so you can encounter all that God has for you!

Okay, this is the question so many ask…"What is the Glory of God?" To simply put it…it is the expression of Himself in His splendor! An expression of Love! Because that's who He is! His splendor speaks of His brilliance, His grandeur, His magnificence. It is a manifestation of who God is and HE is LOVE!!! I will go into more detail with scriptures in the following chapters.

I have encountered God's Glory in my life and pretty much all of my life that I can remember. I just didn't know that was what it was called. As I got older in life, when I would ask others that I knew about my experiences, especially when the supernatural manifestations of His Glory began, people did not have an answer for me. I'm so grateful for the Holy Bible! It's a Holy Bible, not just a Bible. It's our manuscript to Abundant Life. I Love the Word of God, it is my very Life and Spirit!

{John 6:63} *"It is the spirit that quickeneth; the flesh profiteth nothing: the words that I speak unto you, **they are spirit, and they are life**."*

I want to begin first with telling you that God's Love is greater than anything else in your life. If you do not know His Love and flow with His Love, then you will never have the kind of faith that you need. You see, faith only works by Love.

INTRODUCTION

{Galatians 5:6} *"For in Jesus Christ neither circumcision availeth any thing, nor by uncircumcision; but faith which worketh by love."*

So, Faith and Love are intricately connected. You could say that Faith is put into motion by Love! What I want to make clear to you is that as He has manifested His Love to me, He has revealed His Glory to me. After seeking Him as a child, He began to manifest the Supernatural in my life. He is still doing that today in my life as an adult. His Glory has shown up time after time after time! My prayer for you is that His Glory will begin to show up for you! His Glory is increasing!

CHAPTER ONE

REJECTED AND ABANDONED

I'm going to go back and start at a very early age in my life and share with you how the Glory of God showed up. And then I will share when the Glory Cloud began to show up in my life. No matter what you go through in this life, if you have a relationship with God and love Him, He will work all things together for your good. *"And we know that all things work together for good to them that love God, to them who are the called according to his purpose."* {Romans 8:28}

I was born and grew up in Texas. We moved to Oklahoma for a couple of years and then we moved back to Texas and that is where I have lived since. As a young baby, at the age of eighteen months old, my father sexually abused me. He left my mother, my sister, and me. He moved to California when I was three and lived there until he passed away. He never supported me financially, never sent birthday cards, Christmas cards, and he never called me. It was like I didn't exist, like he didn't have a daughter. One day my sister and I came home from school and there was a silver corvette sitting in the driveway with a California license plate. My sister and I thought, who do we know from California that has a corvette? We went straight to our bedroom when we walked into the house. Our mother came into the bedroom and told us that she wanted us to come into the living room and meet our father. I remember feeling like my jaw had dropped to the floor. This man who looked so Indian, because he was, had a beaded headband on and his long, braided hair was down to the middle of his back. And this beautiful woman with long blonde hair. It was a very awkward moment. I didn't like it when he hugged me, and I felt something that did not feel good or right. I was ready to leave the room and didn't want to be around him. And I didn't really know why, either, until God revealed it to me many years later in my early thirties.

I must share this part of the story with you. My father ended up coming to my sister's wedding in 1975. I wanted to know him and about him by this time in my life. So, I asked my father if I could go back to California with him and bring a friend with me. He said I could come and bring my friend, but it was a long ride to California for three people to ride in a two-seater Porsche 911! At that time, of course, I was much smaller than I am today! Ha! So, we all fit just fine!

We made it to California and when we did, it was breakfast time and my father had no breakfast foods to eat. He said he was going to go to the store and when he got back, we would eat and then he would take us to the beach. You can't go to California and not go to the beach! Next thing I knew, one hour had gone by, two hours, finally six hours and I felt sick at my stomach. He never came back! I was experiencing the same feelings of rejection, abandonment and fear all over again that I had when I was a baby and a toddler. I found a phone number of a girlfriend of his and called her. She came and got us, fed us and put us on a plane back to Texas. I did not hear from my father again until I was in my early thirties.

When my father began to contact me in my thirties, God took me through deliverance. He showed me what had happened to me, blanketed me with His Love, He delivered me and healed my soul. (My soul, which is my mind, will and emotions.) Once God delivers and heals you, you must learn to walk it out. Little did I know that the same spirit operating through my father that abused me as a baby would try to manifest its ugly self in my life again. I'm married at this time and with children. My husband traveled all the time and was gone every week. So, I had to really rely and depend upon God to help me. I could not lean upon the arm of man. There are some things in your life that you will learn, only God can bring you through it. Others cannot! My father was an alcoholic and he would call me during the middle of night. There is a two-hour time difference between California and Texas, so when he called me, it was always in the middle of the night and I was asleep. Fear would grip every part of me and I would become totally paralyzed. That is what fear will do to you. I would cry out to the Lord and one day the Lord told me that I would need to confront my father and let him know that he could no longer call me in the middle of the night drunk, defiling me and my family. I remember telling my father, *"You might be my birth father and I love you, but as far as I am concerned right now, you and I do not have a relationship!"* That's just the way it was. Notice that I did not tell him that we couldn't ever have a relationship, I just let him know that we didn't have one at this time. I obeyed what the Lord had told me to do. I had to draw the line and that is what you must do as well. People will only do to you what you allow them to do. You must put your foot down, as they say, and declare these words, NO MORE!

After I told my father that he could not call in the middle of night drunk anymore, he didn't call back for almost two years. The day came again that he called me and this time it was in the middle of the day. I knew that he had not been drinking. We began to talk and from that day we had many conversations during the daytime. He was always encouraging me to eat healthy and exercise. I was so grateful to God that he played golf a lot and ran in several marathon's. You see, I had prayed often and reminded the Lord of His Word that said if there was one in the household that was saved, the whole household would be saved. {Acts 16:31 HCSB} *So they said, "Believe on the Lord Jesus, and you will be saved—you and your household."* But you must understand that every person must believe as well. During the next several years, from time to time, when I would talk to my father about God and Jesus, he wanted nothing to do with them. He told me to believe in my God and he would believe in the sun, the moon and the stars. I quit saying anything to him and kept standing on Acts 16:31. The scripture I mentioned above. Although my father had abused me, abandoned me, rejected me, and had nothing to do with me growing up, I still did not want him to spend eternity in hell.

I believe God gave my father the desire to be healthy since he was an alcoholic. And that kept him until that day came in March of 2006 when he accepted the Lord as his personal Savior. He had been diagnosed with cancer and it was not good. He quit drinking and began to change his life. He was looking for answers. I'll never forget the day that we were talking on the phone and I asked him if he wanted to spend eternity in Heaven. He said "Yes", and I got to lead him to the Lord. I would have never thought or dreamt that I would have been the one, after all, I lived in Texas and he lived in California. I had always prayed, *"God, put someone on his pathway to tell him about You and Jesus, that will lead him to salvation."* It was such an honor for me to lead him to the Lord. He was immediately captivated by the Father's Love and said that he didn't know why he had waited so long to accept Jesus Christ into his life, except that he was stubborn. He said that there was no beer, liquor, or medicines that ever made him feel the way he felt when he accepted Jesus Christ into his life and encountered God's presence and His Glory! To God be all the Glory and Honor and Praise!

LIVING IN VICTORY THROUGH FORGIVENESS

As I shared in the beginning, my testimony is not just about being a victim and becoming victorious. It's about what happens when you walk in the Power of Forgiveness and the Love of God! This testimony is about God's Glory manifesting to my father who was an abusive man, an alcoholic for over sixty years and wanted to have nothing to do with God or Jesus, much less the Holy Spirit! When you forgive and stay in that forgiveness and walk in a spirit of love, God's Glory will show up! And when it does, a miracle is going to happen! There's more to this story about what happened when God's manifested

Glory showed up. Let's continue with what happened just a few weeks later.

My father had been diagnosed with cancer and was getting worse. I was blessed and honored to spend the last week of my father's life with him in a hospice hospital in the mountains of Poway, California. It was such an amazing week that has impacted my life for souls ever since! I pray that you are inspired by it. I'm telling you, I really believe that none of this would have happened if I had not forgiven my father and chosen to walk in a spirit of Love towards him. (Remember, just because you forgive someone and love them does not mean you approve of what they are doing that is contrary to the Word of God.)

I had to choose to forgive my father and walk in the Love of God towards my father. When you choose to forgive, there is a power of God that is released in and through you. And when you walk in the Love of God along with Forgiveness towards someone, you invite the Glory of God to manifest in your life. The Glory of God is miraculous! Because only God can cause what is impossible to manifest. We must walk in the Glory of God today! The Anointing is holy and it's amazing, but it's not enough for today. We work the Anointing with the Holy Spirit, but when the Glory of God shows up, God does it! It's all of Him without you or me!

SALVATION RELEASED

Here's the next part of my story and it's so amazing. God is so good. This is what happened the last week that I was with him. The hospice hospital where my father was staying was in a Filipino community. When I went to my father's room, every day I would put on a

Christian CD and it changed the atmosphere in his room. It was such a blessing because it never bothered his roommate. When you walked into my father's room, it was different from any other place that I went in the hospital. And when others came into his room, they knew it, even a few of his friends that came to say their goodbyes. The second day, one of his nurses came in and asked me if I was a Christian and I told her "Yes!" She asked me if I could pray for her. She was waiting on the deed papers to her home that she had not received from her husband in over a year. I told her that I would be glad to pray for her. I love how the Holy Spirit knows exactly what a person needs to bring them into the Kingdom of God. I told her that first I needed to ask her if she knew Jesus Christ and then for us to pray in agreement, she needed to know Him. Of course, immediately, she said she wanted to know Jesus!

We were sitting at the end of my father's bed on some chairs. My father was not saying much at that time, as he was in the place of transition. But the moment I led her in the Salvation Prayer, my father opened his eyes and lifted his hands to heaven. He was never in church, so please understand what this did to me. I was so amazed. I knew that my father was a new creature in Christ. His spirit man was praising God as a soul was coming into the Kingdom of God. It was such a beautiful thing to see. My heart was overwhelmed with his nurse getting saved, but then to see my father's eyes open and lifting his hands up to the Lord was *the sprinkles on the icing of a cake*, as they say. My father never said anything, he would just close his eyes back and put his hands down afterwards. After she accepted the Lord, her head dropped down and she kept it in that position for several minutes. I went on ahead and prayed with her in agreement for the papers although she was under the influence of the Anointing. Several minutes later, a nurse walking down the hallway was calling out her name and she suddenly lifted her head up, thanked me and said, "Oh, I better get back to work."

The next day when I had come back after going to lunch, she was at the nurse's station. She was glowing, but after all, she had just accepted Jesus Christ into her heart the night before. She smiled at me and asked if she could come down to my father's room and talk to me for a few minutes. I said, "Sure!" She came down later and the very first thing she said to me was, "The deed papers came in the mail this morning!" I was so in awe of God and knew that angels had gotten those papers and put them in the mailbox. She then proceeded to tell me that she had a friend, who was also a nurse there, that wanted me to pray for her because she wanted to know Jesus Christ as her Lord and Savior too. I didn't know how to contain the joy that I felt at that moment. I thought to myself, revival is breaking out in this place. The Glory of God showed up and miraculous things were happening that no man could take the credit. She asked if they could come down after their shift that night. And you know what I said, a big "Yes!" I was so excited I could hardly wait for them to come to my father's room that night. It was an awesome afternoon as I prepared myself for another person coming into the Kingdom and whatever the Lord had ordained.

Their shift had come to an end and they came to my father's room. This is what happened next. After they walked in, I didn't want to disturb my father's roommate, so I walked over to pull the curtain between their beds. When I started to pull the curtain, my father's roommate said to me, "No, not pull curtain!" I almost felt like doing cartwheels. I knew that Father God had been wooing him unto Himself. We got some chairs, sat down and I began to pray with the other nurse. As she was receiving Jesus Christ as her Lord and Savior, it happened again, I looked at my father and there he was lifting his hands to heaven with his eyes open. And as soon as we were finished praying, he closed his eyes and put his hands down. The nurse almost immediately started laughing after she accepted Jesus Christ and she continued to laugh. She could not stop, she was so happy! Some would call it, Holy Ghost laughter. The Holy Bible tells us that the Joy of the Lord is our strength. *"…for the joy of the Lord is your strength."* {Nehemiah 8:10d} Now, if you had seen this precious nurse the day before, she was very sad with her head hanging down and her face was filled with pain and sorrow. But she met Jesus Christ and was instantly changed in His Holy presence. God had given her a new-found strength that she had not ever known. It was such a glorious moment to experience. But hold on, there's something else, the last part of my story that is about God's Glory!

The two nurses got up and they left. So many people have been taught, just as I had been, that we go to church. We go to a place, an edifice, someone's home; but we are the church of the Living God. Always remember that, you and I are the church and we must live and act as the church. Wherever we are, God will use us if we are a yielded vessel. As soon as I turned around and came back into my father's room, I was looking at my father's roommate (who was eighty-five years old) and this precious man's soul was looking at me through his eyes, as he had been watching everything that had just happened. I know he took notes the night before as well. I looked at him, called out his name and asked him if he wanted to know Jesus Christ as his Lord and Savior too! He answered with a big yes!!! I walked over to his bed and took his hands and we prayed through the prayer of Salvation. He had tears flowing down his cheeks. And then, suddenly, he let go of my hand and pointed up into the air with his right pointer finger and said, "I see a light!" I told him that Jesus was the Light of the world and that Jesus was revealing Himself to him. He still had tears coming down his cheeks. It was just so precious. He grabbed my hand and told me something that has changed my life forever concerning souls. He looked at me while holding my hand and said, "You are an angel that God sent to me today. I have been waiting for this day all my life." I was taken back by his words and didn't know what to think about them. I had never heard those words after leading someone to the Lord. And I have led a lot of people to the Lord in my life, but not near as many as I'm going to in the days to come! When I left the hospital that night, I asked Abba Father, how could someone even know to say such a statement like that? And God's response to me was, "Because every person that I create is made to know their Creator and to have a relationship with Me!" I'm telling you, a fire has burned deep within me ever since that day on March 31, 2006 for souls once again. I asked myself, how could this trip have been any better? One seed (my father's life) going into the ground and three seeds (my father's two nurses and roommate) springing up, souls coming into the Kingdom! Ask God to give you a heart for souls and He will.

As I shared with you earlier, this is the first manifestation of God's Glory that showed up in my life. What a miracle of God! My father, that was abusive in many ways, who was an alcoholic for over sixty years of his life and wanted nothing to do with God, changed by God's Glory and got saved! My father came to the place of encountering the Glory of God through being shown Forgiveness and Love! No matter how impossible it looks with someone, God's Glory will always manifest a miracle! Always! Next, one of my father's nurses got saved and angels brought the title deed to her home and put it in her mailbox the next day! Another nurse got saved and joy filled her heart. She had a bounce in her step when she walked and no longer hung her head down! Then my father's eighty-five-year-old roommate got saved and saw a Light, which was a manifestation of Jesus! Wow!! These are some pretty powerful miracles that happened! Praise God for His Glory revealed!

CHAPTER TWO

NEW CREATURES IN CHRIST

There's another manifestation of God's Glory that I am going to be sharing with you in the next several chapters. In this chapter, I want to share a few things to help you before I begin to share the stories with you.

This manifestation of God's Glory is called the Glory Cloud. But remember, God's Glory is intrinsic (belonging to the real nature of a thing) and an expression of His Love! Several places in the Word of God this manifestation shows up.

And guess what? If it showed up in the stories that we read in the Holy Bible and it has shown up in my life, it will show up for you too! I am going to share with you, stories in the following chapters of this book how the Glory Cloud has showed up time and time again and how it lingers in our home and at the church (Church of His Glory) my husband and I co-pastor. This has been happening for over twenty-five years and probably longer, I just didn't realize it!

What I want you, as the reader to understand, is that if you are a born-again believer, you have access to the things of the Spirit. You have accepted Jesus Christ as your Lord and Savior, as I shared in Chapter One, you have been changed, translated from the Kingdom of Darkness into the Kingdom of Light. You are spirit and I am spirit. I always teach this everywhere I go as I stand in a place where everyone can see me, I tell others, "What you see of me right here is not who I am, what you are seeing is only what I like to wear. And if you try to know me by what I wear, by the car I drive, my profession or by my abilities then you will never know me. If you want to know me, you must know me after the spirit, because that is who I am. The Holy Bible teaches us to know no man after the flesh. Remember, I am spirit and you are spirit!"

{2 Corinthians 5:15-17} *"And that he died for all, that they which live should not henceforth live unto themselves, but unto him which died for them, and rose again. Wherefore henceforth know we no man after the flesh: yea, though we have known Christ after the flesh, yet now henceforth know we him no more. Therefore if any man be in Christ, he is a new creature: old things are passed away; behold, all things are become new."*

These three scriptures are letting us know that we are no longer the same and we have become new creatures in Christ. We are no longer living for ourselves as the Word of God says, but for Him. As we walk in the Word of God, we reveal the Spirit of God. You can have as much of God in your life as you want. I want all that I can have so that He will be glorified. I don't know about you, but I want what is in Heaven to be manifested here in the earth in my sphere of influence. Remember, we are only strangers passing through.

{Hebrews 13:14} *"For here have we no continuing city, but we seek one to come."*

{John 17:16} *"They are not of the world, even as I am not of the world."* This is not our home.

{Colossians 3:2} *"Set your affection on things above, not on things on the earth."* I'm being restored back to spirit and I'm on my way home! So are you, if you are a born-again believer!

{2 Corinthians 4:15-16} *"For all things are for your sakes, that the abundant grace might through the thanksgiving of many redound to the glory of God. For which cause we faint not: but though our outward man perish, yet the inward man is renewed day by day."* I want a little bit of Heaven to show up in my part of the world!

Now here are a few scriptures that talk about God's Glory before I start sharing some stories with you. There are many more, but these are the ones I am sharing with you for now.

{Exodus 40:34-35} *"Then a cloud covered the tent of the congregation, and the glory of the Lord filled the tabernacle. And Moses was not able to enter into the tent of the congregation, because the cloud abode thereon, and the glory of the Lord filled the tabernacle."*

{Exodus 13:21-22} *"And the Lord went before them by day in a pillar of a cloud, to lead them the way: and by night in a pillar of fire, to give them light; to go by day and night: He took not away the pillar of the cloud by day, nor the pillar of fire by night,* from *before the people."*

{Exodus 24:15-18} *"And Moses went up into the mount, and a cloud covered the mount. And the glory of the Lord abode upon mount Sinai, and the cloud covered it six days: and the seventh day he called unto Moses out of the midst of the cloud. And the sight of the glory of the Lord was like devouring fire on the top of the mount in the eyes of the children of Israel. And Moses went into the midst of the cloud, and gat him up into the mount: and Moses was in the mount forty days and forty nights."*

My prayer is that as you read my stories, you will be inspired to seek God more and to know

Him more! Please keep your heart open and yield your spirit to Holy Spirit. When you believe, you will receive. I may share some things that you have never heard of and you might even find it hard to believe as well.

{1 Corinthians 2:14} *"But the natural man receiveth not the things of the Spirit of God: for they are foolishness unto him: neither can he know them, because they are spiritually discerned."*

God wants to reveal His Glory to you in every way possible. He wants you to know that there is so much more in knowing Him as well as knowing the things of Heaven. We will keep learning throughout our lives, if we have a teachable spirit. Don't ever stop learning. If you do, you will become stagnant. Your life will become boring and you will begin to die spiritually. Just as without food for your body, you will become weak and eventually die from being malnourished. Don't forget that the Word of God is your very life and spirit. I want to be prepared, as much as possible for where I am going to spend eternity, that is in Heaven! And I hope you do too!

CHAPTER THREE

SOLD OUT TO GOD

When I came back to the Lord in 1987 after living in the wilderness for fourteen years, I started living a sold-out life to God alone! My whole walk with the Lord changed. It's like my senses were heightened, both in the natural and in the spiritual realm. I had such a deep hunger for the Lord and for the things of Heaven. I wanted everything I could have that the Holy Bible said I could have, also I wanted to become and do everything the Holy Bible said I could be and do! I was so hungry! Bottom line, day by day, I was getting to know Holy

Spirit more, I was falling in love with Jesus, and learning of God's great love to me in knowing Him as my Heavenly Father. I thought 'Wow!' This is such an amazing life that we are blessed with as a new creature in Christ. Little did I know what my eyes would be opened up to see in the days ahead and how God would reveal Himself to me. {Ephesians 1:17-18} *"That the God of our Lord Jesus Christ, the Father of glory, may give unto you the spirit of wisdom and revelation in the knowledge of him: The eyes of your understanding being enlightened; that ye may know what is the hope of his calling, and what the riches of the glory of his inheritance in the saints."*

I began to spend many hours a day in the presence of God. I was so grateful in my heart and thankful that I could stay home and do so. In fact, I felt very honored, because most of my friends had to work outside their home. Holy Spirit helped me to balance everyday things in my life so that things were not out of order. As a stay-at-home mom, I learned the importance of prioritizing my day, always making sure that my family was taken care of and the housework was caught up! So, when I separated myself unto God to seek Him, there was no place my mind could go in thinking that I needed to get something done. Now, I will say, sometimes, you will be beckoned or summoned by the Lover of your soul, Jesus, to pull away from watching television or other activities with family. Television is a whole lot different today than what it was when my children were growing up. We watched things together. I guess today, it's not as easy with all the darkness that is on television. But there are some good Christian movies and programs to watch together as a family.

As I began to spend time in the presence of God every day, it happened that one day, suddenly, there was a cloud that appeared in my secret place (which was my bedroom.) The more you see God's Glory, it will begin to transform you into His image. I had been thanking God, praising and worshiping Him. I was so aware of the Holy presence of God. I remember my head felt different. It was like the top part of it was missing! My mind did not understand what I was seeing. But my spirit bore witness with the Spirit of God.

{1 Corinthians 2:9-16} *"But as it is written, Eye hath not seen, nor ear heard, neither have entered into the heart of man, the things which God hath prepared for them that love him. But God hath revealed* them *unto us by his Spirit: for the Spirit searcheth all things, yea, the deep things of God. For what man knoweth the things of a man, save the spirit of man which is in him? even so the things of God knoweth no man, but the Spirit of God. Now we have received, not the spirit of the world, but the spirit which is of God; that we might know the things that are freely given to us of God. Which things also we speak, not in the words which man's wisdom teacheth, but which the Holy Ghost teacheth; comparing spiritual things with spiritual. But the natural man receiveth not the things of the Spirit of God: for they are foolishness unto him: neither can he know* them, *because they are spiritually discerned. But he that is spiritual judgeth all things, yet he himself is judged of no man. For who hath known the mind of the Lord, that he may instruct him? But we have the mind of Christ."*

THE GLORY CLOUD MANIFESTING

I looked up and I noticed this cloud above me. You might say it looked smoky and fuzzy. I then began to understand why in certain places where they used smoke machines and what they were calling holy, why it never was to me! (The devil likes to mimic the things of God to seduce you, because he can't duplicate them. So, he'll create a substitute to pervert the things of God.) He doesn't want you tasting and seeing that the Lord is good. {Psalm 34:8} *"O taste and see that the Lord is good: blessed is the man that trusteth in him."*

This cloud was so thick that I couldn't see the ceiling fan or the ceiling. I really didn't know what to think about that, but I knew I was in the presence of God because I felt Him so strongly. I was totally overcome by His presence. I couldn't do anything for minutes accept behold this amazing thing I was seeing and notice how I felt.

{2 Chronicles 5:13-14} *"It came even to pass, as the trumpeters and singers **were** as one, to make one sound to be heard in praising and thanking the Lord; and when they lifted up **their** voice with the trumpets and cymbals and instruments of **musick**,* *and praised the Lord, saying, For he is good; for his mercy **endureth** for ever: that **then** the house was filled with a cloud, **even** the house of the Lord; So that the priests could not stand to minister by reason of the cloud: for the glory of the Lord had filled the house of God."*

I didn't say anything to anyone, not even my family. But every day, this would happen. Again, suddenly, one day the cloud was not only covering my ceiling and ceiling fan, but now it was covering my closet. You couldn't see the frame or the two doors of my closet. I was speechless. But again, my spirit bore witness with what I saw, and I could feel God. As I kept encountering the Glory of God, I realized that no one that I knew ever talked about it and not only that, when I did start to ask some about it, well, let's just say, they didn't know what to say about what I was experiencing. I know they thought I was strange.

Although no one could explain any of what was happening to me, by the grace of God, I did not allow it to keep me from believing what was happening every time I went into my secret place. You must be careful that you don't allow doubt and unbelief to take hold of your heart. As I continued to believe in what God was revealing to me, not just in my secret place, but in the miracles that were happening in my life and other people's lives, it increased my faith. And it caused me to want more of God in my life.

There's a story in the Holy Bible about a man named Lazarus, who was the brother of Mary and Martha. He had a sickness that Jesus told them was not unto death.

{St. John 11:4} "*When Jesus heard that, he said,* **This sickness is not unto death, but for the glory of God, that the Son of God might be glorified thereby.**"

Jesus loved Mary and Martha and their brother Lazarus. Now Mary and Martha were not happy that Jesus didn't come when they thought He should have come. In fact, it was four days later. And by that time, Lazarus was really stinking where they had laid him. It's interesting what Jesus said to Martha when she took Jesus to where his dead body had been laid for four days. Before Martha took away the stone where he laid, Jesus said this to her. {St. John 11:40} **"...Said I not unto thee, that, if thou wouldest believe, thou shouldest see the glory of God?"**

It's very important that you believe. Miracles happened as we read in the Holy Bible and they are still happening today. A miracle says who Jesus is! You will see through the scriptures I'm fixing to share with you that Jesus is the revelation of God's glory to us. These next scriptures are taken from what I call the greatest apostolic prayer that has ever been prayed and ever will be prayed. It's all about God, our Father and Jesus Christ, the Son of God and God's Glory.

{St. John 17:1-4} *"These words spake Jesus, and lifted up his eyes to heaven, and said,* **Father, the hour is come; glorify thy Son, that thy Son also may glorify thee: As thou hast given him power over all flesh, that he should give eternal life to as many as thou hast given him. And this is life eternal, that they might know thee the only true God, and Jesus Christ, whom thou hast sent. I have glorified thee on the earth: I have finished the work which thou gavest me to do**."

{St. John 17:24} **"Father, I will that they also, whom thou hast given me, be with me where I am; that they may behold my glory, which thou hast given me: for thou lovedst me before the foundation of the world."**

When we see the miracles happen, we glorify in God. Probably some of you reading this book, like Moses did in the book of Exodus, you have cried out, "Lord, show me Your Glory." I shared earlier in my book, that many have walked in the leadership, authority and anointing of God. But no longer will that be enough in these last days. We must walk in the Glory of God. We work the anointing, but when the Glory of God shows up, God will manifest a miracle.

CHAPTER FOUR

GOD'S GLORY MANIFESTED IN DARKNESS

I was really involved in the church that we attended in the late 1980's. I had a Ladies Care group and I was a Ladies Care Leader. The church was having a retreat for all the Care Leaders one weekend which consisted of the Ladies Care Leaders, Geographical Care Leaders and Touch Pastors. At the Retreat, all the ladies stayed in this big room of a cabin and then off to the side of this big room was a small room which I shared with two other women.

One of the women, who was over all the Ladies Care Leaders and then her assistant, who was a very good friend of mine. As we got into bed one night, there was such a strong presence of God. We each had our own bed and they were spaced out a little over an arms distance from each other. I was in the middle bed, with the lady over the ministry on the left and then my good friend on the right. When you turned the lights off in the cabin, it was really dark as we were in a very wooded area. So, the lady over the Care Leaders was almost asleep and my friend was still awake, but not saying anything. Suddenly, the Glory Cloud showed up and it lit the room up. I was in awe at what I saw. I turned my head and asked my friend, "Do you see that?" And she asked, "What?" I said, "Don't you see that white cloud?" She responded back to me and said, "No, I don't see anything Diane, it is pitch black in here!" By then, we had carried on so much that the lady over the amazing weekend. And then the encounter that I had with the Glory of God was like the cherry on the icing! Now, remember, at that time, I didn't realize that was the Glory Cloud. I just knew that it was holy, and I was surrounded by God's presence so strongly. So, are you ready to know what happened? When I got back home on Saturday evening, before I was going to bed, I took the band-aid off and guess what? The mole was totally gone!!! Did you hear me? The mole wasn't there, and my skin was as smooth as baby skin. The mole wasn't just not in the band-aid, it was totally gone. You know, it had disappeared! I then remembered the vision that I had while I was praying. I'm telling you, I started rejoicing and praising the Lord. That was indeed a miracle!

DON'T GIVE UP, YOU WILL SEE

As I looked back on this encounter, it helped me to understand that sometimes, other people's eyes have not *yet* been opened to see. My friend didn't see what I saw. Maybe you're thinking right now, I've never seen anything like that or had anything like that happen to me. Don't give up! You will see one day. God will remove the salve from your eyes so that you can see.

{Matthew 5:8} *"Blessed are the pure in heart: for they shall see God."*

{Revelation 3:18} *"I counsel thee to buy of me gold tried in the fire, that thou mayest be rich; and white raiment, that thou mayest be clothed, and* that *the shame of thy nakedness do not appear; and anoint thine eyes with eye-salve, that thou mayest see."*

You must choose Life and keep doing the right thing. The right thing is doing what you learn from the Word of God. Remember that the

Word of God is your very life and spirit. You must believe in His Word and not doubt it.

{St. John 6:63, 64a} *"It is the spirit that quickeneth; the flesh profiteth nothing: the words that I speak unto you,* they *are spirit, and* they *are life. But there are some of you that believe not."*

So, you must obey His Word. After all, we want unbelievers to know that we are disciples of Jesus Christ and we are to make disciples.

AFFIRMATION...

I also learned from this encounter of God's Glory that God has anointed me as a forerunner. A forerunner is one who goes to a place where others are to follow and prepare a way for them; and also, to open the gates. Now, we know that there is only One true Forerunner and that is Jesus Christ. Just as He is the only One true Apostle and Prophet. We are blessed as believers as we read in the book of Ephesians that He honored us with the Five-Fold Ministry.

{Ephesians 4:11-12} *"And he gave some, apostles: and some, prophets; and some, evangelists: and some, pastors and teachers: For the perfecting of the saints, for the work of the ministry, for the edifying of the body of Christ:"*

CHAPTER FIVE

GOD'S GLORY LINGERS

You just never know when the Glory of God is going to show up! But when you have been with Him, in the secret place, I can tell you that His Glory *will show up*! We need to get into the habit every day to present our bodies to God as a living sacrifice. {Romans 12:1} *"I BESEECH you therefore brethren, by the mercies of God, that ye present your bodies a living sacrifice, holy, acceptable unto God, which is your reasonable service."* Because it has for me time after time, as I have shared in a previous chapter. When you become a living sacrifice as the Holy Bible teaches us and you worship Him, the Glory of God will show up! Hold on tight, because I know some of you might be thinking, when have others seen it? I'm glad you have that question in thought. Something that I always teach others is that whatever is going on at home is what will manifest in public. You can't give what you don't have! And that goes either way. What I mean by that, is, if you are having issues that aren't good in your relationship with your spouse or children, sooner or later, it will manifest in the public. You just can't hide things for too long! On the same token, as you seek God, humble yourself, pray and spend time in His Word and worship Him, you will encounter His Glory and you will begin to experience things in the realm of the Spirit of God. And that will eventually manifest in the public.

MY SON'S ENCOUNTER WITH THE GLORY

In 1987, my husband and son had just come from a hunting trip. They were at the front door. Our door had an oval shaped clear beveled glass in it that went from just about the top to the bottom of the door and you could see right into our home. I had been in the presence of God that morning for several hours. I was sitting in a recliner chair to the left side of our living room and when I saw them standing there, I couldn't move or do anything. I literally could not get up. I was stuck in my recliner. My husband was trying to find his keys and was having a hard time doing so. My son looked in at me and said, "There's mom, she's just sitting there, not doing anything." As I said, I could not move. So, I just sat there and eventually my husband found his keys, opened the door and then came into the house. My husband walked by me and went straight into the kitchen to sit everything down on the table. But my son, well, it was a different story. He walks into the living room, stops right in the middle of it and is looking everywhere, all around the whole living room. He then stops, looks at me and says, "Mom, have you been smoking or something? What is all that smoke?" I looked at him and of course, I responded to him and said, "Casey, you know I don't smoke. That's God!" He then went straight over to the sofa and laid down on it and went to sleep. Now some people might say that he was tired from the long drive home and that's why he went to sleep. But for me, I know that He was touched by God and went and laid down and was captivated in his heart by God. After all, my husband had told me that he had slept most of way home from Mississippi! It wasn't like he really was sleepy. It was still early in the day.

After that day, it seemed that my son had a different hunger for the Lord. By the age of seven, he was already saved and baptized with the Holy Ghost and Fire. He began to move in the supernatural. What I mean by that is that he would do things that a kid wouldn't or doesn't normally do. He would be asleep on the sofa and I would be in the kitchen praying and interceding. He would sit up out of his sleep and prophesy the Word of the Lord to me and lay back down and go to sleep. We would be driving home from church and he would fall asleep. He would lay the seat back. Same thing would happen that happened at home. I would be praying, sometimes just talking to the Lord about some things that were heavy on my heart and suddenly he would sit up, speak a word to me from the Lord and go back to sleep.

The word prophesy according to the King James Dictionary means:

1) To foretell future events
2) To predict

3) To utter predictions

4) To make declaration of events to come.

In the Cambridge Dictionary it means:

1) To say what will happen in the future.

He was very sensitive about the things of God and that sensitivity increased in the days and months to come. I saw that how resting in the Glory of the Lord that day for about three to four hours changed his life personally. You can't help but be changed in the Glory and by the Glory of God.

OTHER PEOPLE'S ENCOUNTER WITH THE GLORY

One time, a friend had come over and when she walked into our home, she took a few steps and stopped (almost like what our son did that day when he walked into the living room) and tears began to stream down her face. She said she didn't know why she was crying, but she felt so much peace. God healed her heart that day as we sat in my living room and talked about the things of God.

Just a few months ago, last year, in 2017. We had family and friends over for Christmas dinner. As I brought one of our friends back into the computer room and we were talking, she told me that she loved being in our home. I'm thinking to myself at first, but our home is just a small home. I told her, "I know you're used to being in really big homes with several square feet and our home is just a very small home." She responded back to me, "I love your home. I love the feeling in your home. It's inviting and feels good. I would rather be in a home this size and feel what I feel, than to be in a big home and not feel this." My heart was overflowing with joy and with gratefulness because I knew that she could feel the presence of God from His lingering Glory that resides in our home.

Also, our precious granddaughter, Maddie, told me just recently, about four weeks ago that she loves coming to our home. I said, "You do?" That's a blessing when your grandchildren like coming to your home. She said, "Yeah, it just feels good in your home, it's like an instant happiness that you feel." Once again, I knew that God's Glory is changing people still as they come into our home. God gets all the glory always!

One night at the church I had just turned out the lights in the sanctuary, getting ready to leave. My secretary, Gena, was in the back turning off all the lights. Suddenly, I felt the Presence of God intensify. I turned around and looked in the sanctuary. On the right side of the platform, the Glory Cloud was manifested. That whole side was lit up like there were lights on…it was amazing! (I had just turned all the lights off and it was pitch black in the sanctuary.) I just stood there in awe of God's Glory. Gena came into the foyer area and was getting ready to turn the alarm on and I told her to come over to where I was standing. I then told her to look into the sanctuary and to the right side of the platform. As soon as I did, she looked in there and immediately started to weep as she fell to the ground bowed over. Her life was changed in those few moments and has never been the same.

CHAPTER SIX

A CHANGED HEART FOR SOULS

Now in this chapter I want to share a story about God's Glory that manifested when my mother had passed away. Remember how I shared in Chapter One, how after leading my father's two nurses and roommate to the Lord that a fire has burned deep within me ever since for souls? Well, what happened concerning my mother's passing was another part of how God was revealing His Glory to me, but also, how it changed my heart for souls!

FEELING DEATH AND THE GLORY MANIFESTING

My precious mother had appointed me to take care of her affairs. So, I had to make decisions about many different things regarding her circumstances when she was no longer able to do so, but also, I had to make all the arrangements after she passed. I stayed before the Lord as much as I could and still separated myself to be in the secret place with Him during this time. After my mother had passed, the funeral home had called me because they wanted me to come and make sure she looked okay for the viewing. I really didn't want to do that, because I never liked that part of a person's passing to begin with, you know going to see their dead body at the viewing the night before the day of the actual Homegoing. It's not the person to begin with, it's just a shell that we recognized as their body. Anyway, when I got there, a lady took me into the room where they had my mother in the casket. It was open and when I looked at my mother, I started feeling a strange feeling. I almost passed out and I had to immediately get out of the room. I just could not be in there any longer. I had only been in there for a few minutes, but it was long enough for me to know that I didn't want to be around death or the dead! As I opened the door, the lady that had taken me back just happened to be walking by and when she saw me, she said, "Mrs. Nutt, are you okay? Why don't you sit down over here and let me go get you some water? You're pretty flushed looking." I said, "I don't feel right, and some water would be great." I sat down and she brought the water and told me to just sit there as long as I needed to before I got up to leave. So, that is exactly what I did. As I took a few sips of water, I began to feel good again. I finally got up to leave and headed home.

When I got home, it was dark by then and I ate just a little bit of dinner. I remember going into my bedroom and just sitting there. It was so much to take in to begin with, knowing that my precious mother would no longer be around. Having the responsibility that I had of doing everything and knowing that I was doing the right thing was on my mind. But I knew that it was about to all be over with. As I was sitting in my room, I had turned the light off. When I did, because we live out in the country, it got dark real quick. Suddenly, I felt very uncomfortable. I felt several different mixed emotions. Emotions that I had not felt at any point of this whole process with my mother that I was going through. I started feeling totally broken, I could feel darkness all around me and not because it was dark in the room. I felt lifeless, hopeless, sadness, depression, helpless and just void, an emptiness that I couldn't relate to at all in the previous days of my life. I thought to myself, why am I feeling like this? This is horrible. I mean it felt like the life had been sucked right out of me. I felt nothing at all. I started crying out to God in such despair, I told the Lord that I couldn't live like this and to please help me.

{Jonah 2:2 NIV} He said: *"In my distress I called to the LORD, and he answered me. From deep in the realm of the dead I called for help, and you listened to my cry."*

{Acts 2:21} *"And it shall come to pass* that *whosoever shall call on the name of the Lord shall be saved."*

And right after I cried out to the Lord, it was instantaneously, as I'm sitting there in the darkness, the Glory Cloud appeared and the whole room lit up! And in that moment, I felt God, I felt like I was alive again. I had hope and I felt like my life had purpose again. My heart was whole feeling. I felt peace, comfort and joy.

I could feel the abundant life of Christ in me again. It was so amazing!

The wonderful truth about God is that when we feel that He is so far away, He is indeed with us. When it feels like we are lost in the darkness, God is really with us.

{I Kings 8:12} *"Then spake Solomon, The Lord said the He would dwell in the thick darkness."*

{Hebrews 13:5b} "For He hath said, I will never leave thee, nor forsake thee."

Now I'm going to connect with how I began this chapter and pull all this together. I want you to see what happened as the Glory of God showed up and how it changed my life. As I had said, there was a fire that began to burn deep within me for souls when I watched how God's Glory had showed up and saw the salvations that took place as my father was transitioning to Heaven. And now with my mother, I got a big reminder of what it feels like to not be saved, to not know Jesus. I felt the death in the room where my mother was when I went to see her body to make sure I was satisfied with what they had done. When a person is not saved, their spirit has no life in it. She was dead, and I felt no life in the room with her. All those mixed emotions I felt at home in my bedroom sitting there in the darkness was a definite reminder of being lost. Even when you've been saved, you go through times of being in the wilderness or the desert and you feel lost. Sometimes, when you've been saved for a long time, you can easily forget where you came from and what it was like when you didn't have Jesus in your life. We must always stay humble knowing that it was by His grace that we were saved. When you forget, you can end up not moving in the compassion of the Lord. Also, you can have an attitude towards sinners and unbelievers when you forget where you came from and how much in need you were of a Savior. Jesus was always moved with compassion for the lost and the hurting. {Matthew 9:36} *"But when he saw the multitudes, he was moved with compassion on them, because they fainted, and were scattered abroad, as sheep having no shepherd."*

Jesus was always helping others and He was always moved with compassion. We should be moved with that same compassion that He has towards us. We are about to see the greatest influx of souls coming into the Kingdom. We must be prepared. We must be ready to help all those who need help in whatever way that might be.

Compassion in the dictionary means to have a deep awareness of the suffering of another coupled with the wish to relieve it. Webster defines the word "Compassion" as; "Pity or Sympathy." Compassion is an active thing. You see someone suffering with something and then you do something about it.

When you start moving in compassion, you can't allow someone that you're around to influence you to not be active and flow in compassion as Jesus would. I'm going to give you an example that hopefully, you can learn from.

GRIEVING THE HOLY SPIRIT

One time I was at the mall with someone and we were walking by the Food Court where some people were sitting at a table. About that time, a young girl in her early twenties started having a convulsion. My heart went out to her. I could feel the compassion stirring in my heart.

{St Matthew 14:14} *"And Jesus went forth, and saw a great multitude, and was moved with compassion toward them, and he healed their sick."*

I walked past her just a little bit and was looking back at her, knowing I needed to do something. The sad thing was that I somewhat ignored it as I turned around and looked at the person that I was with trying to communicate to them that I needed to do something. They were encouraging me to come on, to walk away from what I was seeing. And guess what, I did that, I walked away. I'll never forget the horrible feeling that I felt, knowing that the compassion of the Lord was stirring in me. I walked away because I allowed someone to influence me. My heart felt like it dropped to the floor and it took a while to break through what I felt. I knew that I had grieved the Holy Spirit. That is the worst feeling of all. I don't want to ever grieve Him.

{Ephesians 4:30} *"And grieve not the Holy Spirit of God, whereby ye are sealed unto the day of redemption."*

We probably have all fallen short in this area. I'm so grateful that God is so forgiving and that He will move on us again with His compassion to reach out to others in need. Below is a great scripture text in the Word of God that reveals to us the compassion that a person had for someone.

{Luke 10:30-35} *"And Jesus answering said,* **A certain** *man* **went down from Jerusalem to Jericho, and fell among thieves, which stripped him of his raiment, and wounded** *him,* and departed, leaving *him* half dead. And by chance there came down a certain priest that way: and when he saw him, he passed by on the other side. And likewise a Levite, when he was at the place, came and looked *on him*, and passed by on the other side. But a certain Samaritan, as he journeyed, came where he was: and when he saw him, he had compassion *on him,* And went to *him,* and bound up his wounds, pouring in oil and wine: and set him on his own beast, and brought him an inn, and took care of him. And on the morrow when he departed, he took out two pence, and gave *them* to the host, and said unto him, Take care of him; and whatsoever thou spendest more, when I come again, I will repay thee."

GOD'S GLORY CHANGES YOU

There's a story in the book of Mark in chapter five that talks about a young man who was not in his right mind. They could do nothing with him, they couldn't even tame him. He was in the mountains and in the tombs day after day and he was crying and cutting himself with stones. And then the Bible says that when he saw Jesus coming, he ran to Jesus and began to worship Him. He wondered what Jesus wanted with Him and even asked Jesus why He came to him and to please not torment him. Jesus spoke to the unclean spirit and told it to come out of him. When the devils came out of the young man, they asked to be sent into the swine. Jesus allowed the unclean spirits to do so and all the swine ran off a steep place and fell into the sea where they were choked in the sea. The young man was free. When the people that had been feeding the swine saw this, they went into the city and told everyone. When they came out to the place where this happened, they were afraid when they saw this young man who had been possessed with the devil. He was sitting there still, clothed and in his right mind. Jesus was leaving after that and was on the ship where the young man had entered onto. The young man wanted to go with Jesus and this is what Jesus told him.

{St. Mark 5:19} *"Howbeit Jesus suffered him not, but saith unto him,* **Go home to thy friends, and tell them how great things the Lord hath done for thee, and hath had compassion on thee**."

What an awesome God we serve! And what an amazing story of the compassion that God had on this young man who was so bound.

So, all of this came out of that moment in my bedroom when I was in total darkness. Out of the cry of my heart, God's Glory showed up and my life was changed instantly. Every toxic emotion I had of darkness left me instantly. My heart was filled with such compassion for the lost. I will never forget what happened and I continually give God the Glory for once again saving me out of the mental and emotional state that I was in at that moment!

{Luke 10:19} ***"Behold, I give unto you power to tread on serpents and scorpions, and over all the power of the enemy: and nothing shall by any means hurt you."***

Maybe you are going through something right now and you feel some of the things that I mentioned in this chapter: you feel lifeless, hopeless, helpless, emptiness, a void, depression, or sadness. Right now, just ask Jesus to save you and reveal the Father to you. Ask Him to show you His Glory. {Exodus 33:18} *"And he said, I beseech thee, shew me thy glory."*

CHAPTER SEVEN

MANIFESTING GOD'S GLORY

In Chapter Four, I shared about the Glory of God that manifested to me in the night at a retreat for leaders. God is so amazing! Now I am going to share with you a story about what happened at a women's retreat where I ministered. The Glory of God showed up in a big way. But, before I share about this story, I'm going to share with you what happened to me in a place of privacy.

Remember, how I shared with you previously that what happens in your home or in private, is what will manifest in public. You can't give or release what you have not received. This will help you to understand more, why it is so important that you spend quality time in the secret place with God.

WHAT HAPPENED IN PRIVATE

Around 1988, there were a handful of women that I got together with often and prayed. They were part of my Ladies Care Group. We met at different times outside of our regular scheduled meetings and prayed together. We had a strong core group of about five of us.

One night, I had gone over to one of their homes and the two of us were in one of the rooms praying. We had been praying together and then we decided to go to a different part of the room and just pray alone with God by ourselves. As I was down on my knees, knelt by the bed, I remember the presence of God manifesting in a very strong way. Next thing, I knew, the Glory of God had shown up. I had been pouring my heart out to the Lord, presenting my body as a living sacrifice to the Lord.

{Romans 12:1-2} *"I BESEECH you therefore, brethren, by the mercies of God, that ye present your bodies a living sacrifice, holy, acceptable unto God, which is your reasonable service. And be not conformed to this world: but be ye transformed by the renewing of your mind, that ye may prove what **is** that good, and acceptable, and perfect, will of God."*

There was a very sweet fragrance that you could smell in the room and as I looked over to the side of the room, there was smoke that was rising up. You could literally see and smell incense! Now remember, I had been pouring my heart out to the Lord. Laying many things on the altar.

{Leviticus 16:12-13} *"And he shall take a censer full of burning coals of fire from off the altar before the Lord, and his hands full of sweet incense beaten small, and bring* it *within the vail: And he shall put the incense upon the fire before the Lord, that the cloud of the incense may cover the mercy seat that* is *upon the testimony, that he die not:"*

{Exodus 40:26-27} *"And he put the golden altar in the tent of the congregation before the vail: And he burnt sweet incense thereon; as the Lord commanded Moses."*

{Leviticus 1:17} *"And he shall cleave it with the wings thereof, but shall not divide it asunder: and the priest shall burn it upon the altar, upon the wood that **is** upon the fire: it is a burnt sacrifice, an offering made by fire, of a sweet savour the Lord."*

Now, you might be thinking: what does this mean, all this sacrifice stuff? We don't sacrifice animals today, but we sacrifice our lives, our bodies and possessions to the Lord. We initially give up our rights when Jesus becomes the Lord of our lives. And we surrender to His will, His Holy Word. Now, He does give us free will to choose. The Holy Bible says that obedience is better than sacrifice. Sometimes in the place of obedience, we find ourselves having to make a sacrifice. Let me share with you what the word *'sacrifice'* means.

According to the Dictionary it means:

1) An act of slaughtering an animal or person or surrendering a possession as an offering to God or to a divine supernatural figure.

2) An animal, person, or object offered in a sacrifice.

3) An act of giving up something valued for the sake of something else regarded as more important or worthy.

We all, at times, make sacrifices. As I shared with you earlier, we should daily present our bodies to God as a living sacrifice according to Romans 12:1.

What happened next was mind blowing! It is really going to be hard to articulate in words what happened, but I'm going to try my best.

God loves us so much! And He loves to reveal His Glory to us! I want to enlighten you with this: The culture of the Kingdom of God is the Supernatural. When you choose to continue in the Word of God, becoming a disciple, you will encounter the Supernatural power of God. I've heard many ministers say, God will put His Super on your natural.

I had been kneeling on my knees for a good while and felt like I just needed to lay down on the floor. By then, of course, the Glory of God had manifested. I was already in awe of His presence. I felt His Love so strongly and then it literally felt like while I was laying there, I could feel His spirit come into my body, but it was as though I could feel the scars on His hands and feet. I told you that it was going to be hard to articulate in words. This is the best way I know how to explain it. I began to feel the greatest expression of Abundant Life I had ever known within me. Every part of my being was alive and almost exploding with Life!

Galatians 2:20} *"I am crucified with Christ: nevertheless I live; yet not I, but Christ liveth in me: and the life which I now live in the flesh I live by the faith of the Son of God, who loved me, and gave himself for me."*

{Romans 6:6} *"Knowing this, that our old man is crucified with* him, *that the body of sin might be destroyed, that henceforth we should not serve sin."*

It was the most amazing 'oneness' with Christ I have ever experienced in my life. It was as though I was emotionally and mentally healed. My heart no longer felt broken, but it was whole and complete in Christ and I knew it. After that happened to me, when I would minister and still to this day, at different times, people will tell me that when I walk up to them and I'm standing in front of them and begin to pray for them, they feel something step or come into their body. They can feel a power come into their whole being.

And then, of course, after they feel that, they usually are slain in the spirit. In other words, they are no longer able to stand in the Holy presence of God and they fall to the floor. They aren't just touched by the Power of God, but they are eternally changed! To God be all the Glory!

THE WOMEN'S RETREAT

Some of you may be wondering what happened at the women's retreat that I spoke about earlier? Now you will better understand, as I shared with you what happened. It was on a Saturday morning; the last session of the retreat and I was the guest speaker. The Presence of God was already strong, and women were being touched by the Lord as I was sharing the Word of God. After I shared the Word of God, I began to pray for the women. As I went over to where they were and prayed for them, they fell under the Power of God. Now, several women were on the floor and the Holy Spirit was ministering to them. Suddenly, over several of the women that were on the floor, there was incense that was rising over their bodies and the sweetest fragrance was manifesting. I could see the smoke of incense and smell the sweet fragrance, but I wanted to know if anyone else could as well. I turned to my left and looked at the pastor and asked her if she could see or smell anything. She told me yes, that she could smell a sweet fragrance. I then asked the women who were sitting in their chairs if they could see the smoke of the incense and smell the sweet fragrance. Most of the women said that they could, but there were some who didn't. Everyone that could though, was in awe, as it was a very holy moment. God had manifested His Love to these precious women that I had prayed for and they received healing in their hearts and minds.

The English Dictionary tells us that the word *incense* means: a substance that is burned to produce a sweet smell.

When we allow the fire to come and burn everything up and we walk in Love, we become a sweet savor in the nostrils of God.

{Ephesians 5:1-2} *"Be ye therefore followers of God, as dear children; And walk in love, as Christ also hath loved us, and hath given himself for us an offering and a sacrifice to God for a sweet smelling savour."*

You just never know what is going to happen in the Holy presence of a Holy God. If you keep your heart open to the Lord and your soul surrendered, (your soul is your mind, will and emotions) then you will be positioned to partake of the supernatural. God wants you to know what your inheritance is as a child of God. Remember, we are on this journey called life and our mission here on earth is to make disciples. We are preparing ourselves for our eternal home, Heaven. This world is not our home, we are only passing through.

The things I have shared so far in my book are just a few things that I have encountered. I love the Supernatural! I never knew how exciting this life could be surrendered to God. He is so good! He tells us in His Word that He will withhold no good thing from us nor alter the word that He speaks.

{Psalms 84:11} *"For the Lord God **is** a sun and shield: the Lord will give grace and glory: no good* thing *will he withhold from them that walk uprightly."*

CHAPTER EIGHT

TO WALK IN TRUTH OR NOT

I pray this next story that I share with you will impact your heart greatly and will inspire you to not ever hold back from sharing the saving knowledge of Jesus Christ.

{Isaiah 60:1-7} *"Arise, shine; for thy light is come, and the glory of the Lord is risen upon thee. For, behold, the darkness shall cover the earth, and gross darkness the people: but the Lord shall arise upon thee, and his glory shall be seen upon thee. And the Gentiles shall come to thy light, and kings to the brightness of thy rising. Lift up thine eyes around about, and see: all they gather themselves together, they come to thee: thy sons shall come from far, and thy daughters shall be nursed at* thy *side. Then thou shall see, and flow together, and thine heart shall fear, and be enlarged; because the abundance of the sea shall be converted unto thee, the forces of the Gentiles shall come unto thee. The multitude of camels shall cover thee, the dromedaries of Midian and Ephah; all they from Sheba shall come: they shall bring gold and incense; and they shall shew forth the praises of the Lord. All the flocks of Kedar shall be gathered unto thee, the rams of Nebaioth shall minister unto thee: they shall come up with acceptance on mine altar, and I will glorify the house of my glory."*

God desires to pour His Glory out upon us. In the beginning of the scripture text above in Isaiah, that word Arise, means to change position. That is something that you must do. If you are sleeping, then wake up. If you are sitting, then stand up. If you are standing, then begin to walk. If you are walking, then begin to sprint. If you are sprinting, then begin to run. You must change position!

Webster's New World Dictionary definition of arise:

1) To get up, as from sleeping
2) To ascend
3) To come into being
4) To result (from)

We all face moments in our life that we feel trapped and we don't see a way out. The truth is, those are real places that we get into in our lives. Only God can intervene and change us and change the outcome of being in that place. Now sometimes, that place can be an emotional and mental place, it can be a financial place, it can be a broken relationship, it can be a bad marriage, it can be a disobedient child that has gone too far for us, it can be a health situation and it also can be an actual life and death situation. Whatever that place is, we know that if we have given God control of our lives, He will get us through it. It has always amazed me how so many believers say that God is in control. That simply isn't totally true. If we have a free will, how can God be in control in our life if we are not choosing His will? He cannot, and He won't! He will step back and let us do whatever we want to because He will not force His will on anyone. That's why He gave us a free will. If He forced us to obey Him and to choose His will, then His Word would not be true. His Word is true, it's the whole truth and nothing but the truth! Don't deceive yourself and think that God is in control of your life if you're not giving Him your will. Something you might want to confess in the morning when you get up that might be helpful as I've shared with many is: *"I will my will to Your will today, God."* I've taught this to our congregation, on my radio program and wherever I can. We must give it all to Him, fully surrendered to His Will. This will of ours can get in the way and hinder us from our destiny if we allow ourselves to be in control.

In December of 2015, I made my mind up that it was going to be the year that I shared the plan of salvation at our annual family Christmas gathering. Can you think of someone in your family or extended family that you keep thinking year after year, you are going to ask them the question? If you were to die today, where would you spend eternity? For many years, I always thought about it. And then every year after the family gathering, I would be so sad that I didn't share anything. I just wasn't sure about several of them. It doesn't matter if you go to a building every week that you call church and meet with other believers, that isn't what saves you. Nor your good works. It got worse for me as each year passed because my spirit became grieved inside of me. I knew that my extended family needed to know that they were going to spend eternity in either one of these two places, heaven or hell. I don't want any family member end up in hell, when I had the opportunity to share with them the Gospel. I can't imagine standing there on judgement day and one of my family members saying, "Diane, you were a preacher and you never asked me if I knew where I would spend eternity after I died." I would rather be rejected by a family member (or anyone) for sharing the Gospel than grieve the Spirit of God on any day of my life. When you know what is right and you don't do it, it is sin. {James 4:17} *"Therefore to him that knoweth to do good, and doeth* it *not, to him it is sin."* Notice that the Holy Bible says to him it is sin, not to everyone else. That is why you cannot judge others according to what you have been set free from, calling it sin in their life. Until the Holy Spirit brings a conviction of truth, what was sin in your life is not sin in another person's life. A person's life being changed on the inside is because of the work of the Holy Spirit, not because of you or me. Anything that is not of faith is sin. {Romans 14:23b} *"...for whatsoever is not of faith is sin."*

We must believe and not doubt whatever the Word of God says. Trust God that if you obey His Word, you will see the fruit of your obedience and enter into rest. In Romans, chapter 14, the Word of God also tells us that the Kingdom of God is righteousness, peace and joy in the Holy Ghost. God's Kingdom manifested in our life is *rest*. The children of Israel could not enter into their *rest* because they had unbelief in their hearts. If that happened to them, don't you think that our unbelief, which is a lack of faith, can keep us out of our rest? So many times, we look at sin as a result of a weakness of our flesh, right? But it isn't! Don't get me wrong, there is a weakness of our flesh. What is the root of sin, though? The root of sin is "unbelief!" The children of Israel revealed this to us. Unbelief is a lack of faith. {Hebrews 11:6} *"But without faith it is impossible to please him: for he that cometh to God must believe that he is, and that he is a rewarder of them that diligently seek him."*

Having a lack of faith causes us and leads us to produce sin in our life! We must live a life of faith, never doubting what He says. Let me give you a few examples.

CHOOSING SIN

Several years ago, actually, three decades ago, I had been diagnosed with Temporomandibular

Joint Dysfunction known as TMJ. The temporomandibular joint is on both sides of your face. It is the joint that connects your jaw to your skull. The muscles near them allow you to open and close your mouth. If it is injured or damaged, it can lead to a localized pain disorder called TMJ. The causes of TMJ include injury to the teeth or jaw, misalignment of the teeth or jaw, teeth grinding, poor posture, stress, arthritis, and gum chewing. Here's the example now! So, I had been diagnosed with TMJ and I was a habitual gum chewer. Now in the beginning I didn't know that gum chewing was a cause for TMJ. One day in prayer, I heard loud and clear these words, "Diane, quit chewing gum." I thought to myself, what? That's ridiculous, quit chewing gum. Well, guess what, I did not believe that it was the Lord speaking to me. What was that? Unbelief!! And then guess what, the pain got worse and worse. They put me on a pain medication and the TMJ kept manifesting. I was bullheaded as I still hadn't stopped chewing the gum. Finally, one day I put it together and realized that God wasn't being mean to me, He was trying to help me so that I wouldn't be in pain. Now, this is the part that might be hard for you to swallow, kinda like brussel sprouts or any other vegetable that you don't like! Because I had unbelief in my heart. I doubted that God was telling me to quit chewing the gum and it became sin in my life. I'm not saying that chewing gum is a sin. But I knew what was right and I didn't listen and obey God. I was not operating in faith. I suffered the consequences of my sin by not obeying and suffered more pain. That's what Paul was telling the church in the book of Romans, chapter 14 as I shared earlier, when he told them that whatever wasn't of faith was sin.

Before I share what happened at our family Christmas gathering, I must share with you what happened the week before. What did happen the week before changed my life totally and I'm forever grateful for God's mercy and His grace. You will understand why I had made my mind up that the Christmas of 2015 is the year that I was sharing the plan of salvation at the annual family gathering. I was not going to let another year pass me by and be grieved in my spirit once again.

CHAPTER NINE

THE FINGER OF GOD

This is the part of my story that will reveal how the Glory of God showed up and another miracle happened in my life. It was Saturday, exactly one week before the gathering. My husband was out of town and I was out wrapping up my shopping, getting a few things for the next weekend. I had stopped and gotten gas and went inside to pay. On the shelf with candy I saw Atomic Fire Balls. I remembered how good those were, as I got them all the time when I was growing up. So, I bought a few of them and then headed out of the store. As I was driving, sucking on the fire ball, I had a thought, all a sudden, of the fire ball going down my throat. It was a horrible thought to have, but I blew it off and kept driving. Next thing I knew, the fireball had slid down my throat. And it became stuck in my esophagus. Of course, I found a place to pull over and I about started to panic. You must understand, the fire ball was stuck, it wasn't moving. It was not going down at all. I looked in the mirror and I couldn't even see it. I tried to cough it up several times and nothing was happening. As I sat there, I saw my life flash by me and knew that if God didn't intervene, I was fixing to check out of this world, as they say.

In my heart, I was asking God to forgive me of all my sins. I became tense as I began to have muscle spasms. My throat was conforming to the fire ball. I was really afraid as I couldn't talk to even call 911 for help. I started getting really panicky on the inside. The Lord spoke to me and said, "*Diane, Be still!*" I've always shared that He didn't have to tell me that it was Him. I knew who was speaking to me. I got really still and there was a peace that came over me like a blanket, that there was no explanation, except that it was Jesus. The Holy Bible says that God will give you a *peace that passes all understanding.* He heard my plea and sent me comfort through the peace. I was so peaceful and I as I sat there, suddenly I felt the finger of God push that fire ball up my throat and then into my mouth. When I think about it, the only way I could describe or compare the ease of that fire ball coming up my throat would be like a person ice skating. I'm telling you, I never once gagged, choked, or had any kind of reflex. It was absolutely a miracle! There have been some people that hadn't really understood when I've shared this story. They thought I choked on a fire ball. I never once had any kind of natural manifestation as the fire ball was coming up my throat. It was so smooth. The fire ball glided up my throat with no noise. That's not possible as I've been told. I mean, think about it…this is pretty gross to share. If you've ever been sick at your stomach with food poisoning or whatever and you've thrown up, you know how bad that hurts. This did not hurt at all, I was so peaceful. The Glory of God was for sure in my car when this happened.

GIVING GOD CONTROL

Sometimes in life, things can tend to get out of control. We do everything that we know to do and still nothing changes or happens. We must realize that when we have no control in our circumstance, if we have given God control, He will do what only He can do. There in His Glory, a miracle happened once again! This miracle made me really think about how important that it is that we do not put off telling our loved ones or anyone about the Lord. I said in the last chapter, I was not going to let another year go by and be grieved in my spirit. What's worse, is grieving the Holy Spirit. Having a near death experience as this opened my eyes to see once again, that life is like a vapor, here one day and gone the next day. I couldn't bear the thought of not knowing if our family members knew or had even heard that they would be spending eternity in hell or heaven. It wasn't a very easy thing to end up sharing at the Christmas gathering. The enemy put a fight up and tried to shut me down so that I wouldn't say anything. And of course, he did that through a family member that spoke ugly to me as I was beginning to share what had happened the weekend before with the fire ball. But I chose not to be embarrassed or even respond to how I was treated at that moment. I pressed in and shared the story of what happened. And then I told all our family members how much they were loved by God and myself too! I was so relieved afterwards and had such peace in my heart. Now their blood was off my hands. And now it is up to each one of them to make that decision of where they want to spend eternity!

CHAPTER TEN

THE SECRET PLACE

In Chapter Three I shared with you how suddenly there was a cloud that appeared in my secret place. Every day, as I was eager to get into my secret place, God met with me and He revealed His Glory to me and then one day His Glory Cloud appeared. There is something about beholding the beauty of the Holiness of God that gets you hooked on Jesus! The Glory Cloud is holy!

{Psalms 110:3} "Thy people *shall be* willing in the day of thy power, in the beauties of holiness from the womb of the morning: thou hast the dew of thy youth."

This is an amazing scripture and there is so much to it that we need to understand. Let me explain to you what I am talking about. God wants us to go from the place of obedience to having a desire for Him. Yes, obedience is better than sacrifice and has its rewards as the Word of God says. But, what if we lived that life of obedience daily? The apostle Paul said that He died daily. Our hunger and desire for God and the things of God would increase immensely. Our soul would be in subjection to our spirit and our spirit in subjection to the Spirit of God. God's power is being displayed through the obedience of His son, Jesus Christ. Jesus Christ rose from the grave and defeated every foe and captivity captive. He made a public display of Satan's complete defeat! And now, today, Jesus is sitting at the right hand of the Father and all His enemies are being put under our feet. Don't ever forget, He defeated them all! There is no enemy that you and I will ever face that has not been defeated. *"Hallelujah, somebody rejoice right now!"* That is such good news to know that the battle with Satan has already been won and through our obedience, we maintain that victory. Remember though, that God desires *relationship* with us! When I fell in love with my husband, I desired to be with him more and more as time went by. I desired that time and fellowship with him. As we have gone through the ups and downs of all these years (forty-two years at the writing of this book) we have learned a secret to keeping peace in our marriage. "Every disagreement that we have has already been won!" The enemy wants us to argue, fight and be upset with each other so that we grow apart and don't want to be around each other. His plan is to separate and divide us.

But God wants us to grow and become closer and stronger in our relationship, knowing that whatever we might face in our relationship, Jesus overcame it when He took the keys from Satan. Jesus Christ made a public display of Satan in every area that we deal with today, including our relationship with our spouses or anyone. I hope you are beginning to understand what I am talking about here as far as developing a *desire* for God. When you learn to be obedient to God's Word, then less of your flesh gets in the way. The less of your flesh that is manifesting, the more you are in the spirit.

{John 3:30} *"He must increase, but I must decrease."*

Remember how I said in the beginning of this chapter, that every day I was eager to get into *my secret place*? I began to *desire* Him more and more. The more you get to know Him, the more you want to know Him and the more you desire Him. I wanted to behold the beauty of His holiness and I still do today. The Holy Bible tells us to be holy because He is holy. Also, the Holy Bible tells us that the pure in heart will see God.

It's so easy to get away from the *secret place* because we are so busy with the things we do every day. We must discipline ourselves to get into the *Secret Place.* You must make the effort to take time out of your day for Him. He longs to spend time with you in the *secret place* as much as you desire to be in His presence. In fact, He longs for you to want to be with Him in the *secret place.* He so desires to manifest Himself to you, for you to get to know Him. He desires "intimacy!"

DISAPPEARING IN THE GLORY CLOUD

After many years of going into *my secret place* and encountering the Glory of God as well as the Glory Cloud, something amazing took place one day. It was an ordinary day just like any other day that I was seeking God in *my secret place.* Suddenly, the Glory Cloud showed up as it always did, but this time it was so thick. It was thicker than I had ever seen it. I was overtaken by the Presence of God. Now this always happened, but this particular time, it was on a whole new level. The Glory began to move down the left wall in *my secret place.* It moved all the way down the wall until it had come to the corner of the other wall. Then the Glory Cloud began to move across my room until it stopped where I was sitting on my bed. Now I want you to get a good visual of what I am saying. I'm sitting on the right side of my bed and the Glory Cloud was next to me on my left side, going down the middle of my bed from the wall behind the headboard of my bed all the way across the room to the other side. You could see nothing on the left side of my room. On that side of the room was the door that came into our bedroom, the left side of our closet door and then our Chester Drawers. Our Chester Drawers has fourteen drawers and is very tall. I have to stand on my tip-toes to reach the back of the top of it. It had all disappeared in the Glory Cloud. I was so in awe. It was one of those moments that you are speechless. Because I've read in the Word of God where the Glory Cloud showed up and the priests could not minister as I shared with you in Chapter Three. As I sat there, I really wanted to know about this thick cloud that was right next to me. I decided to stick my hand and arm in it. What happened next, was beyond my comprehension. Beyond anything that I could have ever thought or imagined. My hand and forearm up to my elbow disappeared in the Glory Cloud. I pulled my arm out quickly, took my right hand and put in front of my face, practically touching my nose to see if I still had a hand. I know that probably sounds crazy, but just wait until you encounter His Glory like that!

I know that you might find this hard to believe, but it is scriptural. I have shared scriptures in the previous chapters that tell you so. I then stuck my arm in the Glory Cloud again. After doing it about three or four times, I asked God why He was showing me this. He did not answer. I sat there in His presence and then decided to stick my arm in the Glory cloud again. I did it a few more times. By then, I was so overtaken by God's Glory, His presence and His love that I was couldn't do anything. I asked Him again, why He was showing me this. I was so humbled and honored, because of His holiness that I was aware of at that moment. I told Him how grateful I was every time He showed me the Supernatural. I knew that it was always for a righteous cause.

This time He responded to me and said, ***"Diane, as long as you read My Word, pray and worship Me; when I send you before others, they will not see you, but they will see Me. No flesh will glory in My Presence."*** Wow, I was totally wrecked by then. I cried and cried. Tears of gratefulness that He would allow me to encounter His Glory Cloud on that level and letting me know that as I obeyed what He said to me, that others would see Him and not me. It was only a week after that when someone in the service when I was ministering came up to me afterwards and told me that while I was ministering that the top part of my body disappeared and all they could see was a white cloud. Others came and said they saw a gold cloud. And until this day at this writing, people tell me quiet often, that they can't see me any longer after I start ministering. They hear Jesus and some see Jesus. Just recently, a young man, Michael, says that when I'm in the pulpit preaching, I look different. He said that I have a golden glow around me and my skin is smooth and clean and my hair is different. And then he said that when I am speaking prophetically, there is a heavy cloud that surrounds me and emanates as I begin to speak. His life has been changed because of seeing that and He has been inspired to know God more.

This is what we want is for others to see Him in us. There will come a day when believers are gathered together, and we will not be able to stand, we will not be able to be seen, and others will not be able to enter the room because of the Presence of God's Glory. These supernatural manifestations are not for us, but to point others to God! Our Father is being glorified in and through these manifestations!

CHAPTER ELEVEN

SCRIPTURES

Introduction

John 6:63

Galatians 5:6

Chapter One

Romans 8:28

Acts 16:31 (HCSB)

Nehemiah 8:10d

Chapter Two

2 Corinthians 5:15-17

Hebrews 13:14

John 17:16
Colossians 3:2
2 Corinthians 4:15-16
Exodus 40:34-35
Exodus 13:21-22
Exodus 24:15-18
1 Corinthians 2:14

Chapter Three
Ephesians 1:17-18
1 Corinthians 2:9-16
Psalm 34:8
2 Chronicles 15:13-14
John 11:4
John 11:40
John 17:1-4
John 17:24

SCRIPTURES

Chapter Four

Matthew 5:8

Revelations 3:18

John 6:63, 64a

Ephesians 4:11-12

Chapter Six

Jonah 2:2 (NIV)

Acts 2:21

1 Kings 8:12

Hebrews 13:5b

Matthew 9:36

Matthew 14:14

Ephesians 4:30

Luke 10:30-35

Mark 5:19

Exodus 33:18

Chapter Seven
Romans 12:1-2
Leviticus 16:12-13
Exodus 40:26-27
Galatians 2:20
Romans 6:6
Ephesians 5:1-2
Psalm 84:11

Chapter Eight
Isaiah 60:1-7
James 4:17
Romans 14:23b
Hebrews 11:6

Chapter Nine
Psalm 46:10a
Philippians 4:7

SCRIPTURES

Chapter Ten

Psalms 110:3

John 3:30

All scriptures are from the Authorized King James Version unless otherwise noted

ABOUT THE AUTHOR

Diane Nutt was called of God at a very early age and has triumphantly overcome by the Blood of Jesus and the word of her testimony in many areas of her life. Those areas include: fear, anxiety, rejection, loneliness, abandonment, depression, suicide, drug and alcohol addiction, sexual abuse and sin, arthritis, PMS, and fibromyalgia.

Streams of deliverance and healing flow as she minsters under the Anointing of the Holy Ghost. She operates in the prophetic to warn, to encourage, and to strengthen the Body of Christ. She also operates in the Love of God that draws people in the world as well as born-again believers that changes their lives.

She is mightily being used by God to bring change in the hearts of people. She carries the mantle of an Apostle, as well as a Prophet, and has not only impacted individuals, but whole cities and regions for the Kingdom of God. She has a mandate on her life to bring people into the presence of God, to execute judgement and truth, so the lost will be found, the hurting will be healed and the bound will be set free by the Anointed One—Jesus Christ of Nazareth.

Diane currently oversees Church of His Glory in Rockwall, Texas. She works with her husband, Kenneth, in the ministry there. She is the President/Founder of Dove Ministries since March of 1995. She has birthed a new ministry, Glory Training Center, which is coming together and hopefully will open sometime in the next year. She also hosts a radio program, Dove Ministries of Love, since April of 2010, that is aired all over the world. She has had television

ABOUT THE AUTHOR

programs in the Dallas/Ft Worth Metroplex area in the past. She also has been a guest on Sid Roth's, *It's Supernatural!* as well as other television programs.

She has been married to her husband, Kenneth, for forty-two years. She resides in Rockwall County with her husband where they have lived for the last thirty-five years. They have two children, Jill who is married to Kevin and Casey who is married to Melanie and together they have blessed them with seven grandchildren. Maddie, Haidyn, Caleb, Jude, Brice, Logan and Evan. Diane loves her family and they always come first before ministry. Her grandchildren bring her so much joy. She also has several spiritual sons and daughters that she has mentored and poured into throughout the years and continues to do so.

ANOTHER BOOK BY DIANE NUTT

THIS NUTT'S PATH TO FREEDOM
Choose Life and Not Death

This book shares part of her testimony about supernatural encounters with God. Her journey was a battle of life and death where the enemy wanted to and tried several times to kill her, but God had a purpose and plan for her life that no devil in hell could stop. This book will encourage and challenge you not to give up when life tries to pull you under. It will help you understand that God has a good future for you that can only be found in Jesus Christ.

SOON TO BE RELEASED BOOKS

WALKING IN THE GLORY OF GOD

I hope and pray that you have been changed in your life after reading ***Encountering The Glory of God***. Are you ready for more? In my next book; ***Walking in The Glory of God***, I want to teach you how to walk in the Glory of God. You will see how easy it is to walk in God's Glory. Of course, there is a process that you must go through and continue to walk out as you go from Glory to Glory. There are different realms of God's Glory to encounter as you learned in this book. You can be in meetings or gatherings where the Glory of God and the Glory Cloud is manifesting. And what a blessing that is! But I want you to know that as you learn to encounter God's Glory by going into the Secret Place just as you learned in this book, you will soon release the Glory of God wherever you go. Remember always, you can't give what you haven't received. That's why it's so important for you to keep growing in your walk with God so that you will have something to give to others on a continual basis.

LIVING IN THE GLORY OF GOD

I am so excited about the book following ***Walking in The Glory of God***, which is called ***Living in The Glory of God***. Once you have learned to walk in the Glory, then you can begin to live in the Glory. Isaiah tells us the Glory of God is rising upon us and even through there is darkness covering the earth and gross darkness the people, that His Glory is going to be seen upon us. And then the Gentiles will come to the light and kings will come to the brightness of our rising. Isn't that good new to you? How awesome is that? What an honor and a privilege we have being a part of the Kingdom of God. In my upcoming book, ***Living in The Glory of God***, I will be sharing with you not only stories of my own, but I will be sharing stories of others that have encountered the Glory of God through my ministry. What they did with the Word of God they received and obeyed God, following His instructions in their life.

So be on the lookout for these next two books. Check out my website or Facebook page listed on the contact information page to know the availability of these two books to be released.

CONTACT INFORMATION

For more information about Diane's ministry, products or to partner with her, please contact via the following:

Write: Dove Ministries
P. O. Box 1795
Rockwall, TX 75087

Email: doveminrc@aol.com
diane@dove-ministries.com
Website: www.dove-ministries.com
Facebook: Diane Nutt
Instagram: dianelivesforjc